AMAZING ART FORMS

The Art of Photography

BY DAVID J. CLARKE

Kids Core
An Imprint of Abdo Publishing
abdobooks.com

abdobooks.com

Printed in the United States of America, North Mankato, Minnesota.
102024
012025

THIS BOOK CONTAINS RECYCLED MATERIALS

Cover Photos: Shutterstock Images (camera, scenery)
Interior Photos: Shutterstock Images, 4–5, 6, 9, 16, 17, 18, 28 (bottom), 29 (top), 29 (bottom); David Fitzgerald/Sportsfile/Getty Images, 7; Ihor Koptilin/Shutterstock Images, 10–11; Images By Tang Ming Tung/DigitalVision/Getty Images, 13; iStockphoto, 14, 26; Science & Society Picture Library/Getty Images, 20–21; Larry Colwell/Anthony Barboza/Archive Photos/Getty Images, 23; Hayk Shalunts/Shutterstock Images, 25; Sergey Tinyakov/Shutterstock Images, 28 (top); Kamil Zajaczkowski/Shutterstock Images, 29 (middle)

Editor: Haley Williams
Series Designer: Katharine Hale

Library of Congress Control Number: 2024938377

Publisher's Cataloging-in-Publication Data

Names: Clarke, David J., author.
Title: The art of photography / by David J. Clarke
Description: Minneapolis, Minnesota: ABDO Publishing, 2025 | Series: Amazing art forms | Includes online resources and index.
Identifiers: ISBN 9781098295790 (lib. bdg.) | ISBN 9798384916796 (ebook)
Subjects: LCSH: Art--Juvenile literature. | Photography--Juvenile literature. | Photography, Artistic--Juvenile literature. | Photography, Artistic--History--Juvenile literature. | Photographic lenses--Juvenile literature. | Arts and history--Juvenile literature.
Classification: DDC 770--dc23

CONTENTS

Some people capture photos professionally. Others do it for fun or as a hobby.

CHAPTER 1

Why Pictures Matter

Talia's teacher gave the class an assignment. Everyone had to create a story about something they liked to do. But instead of writing, they would create a photo essay. A photo essay is a way to tell a story with pictures rather than words.

Newer models of some smartphones have three cameras on the back of them. This helps people take better quality photos.

Talia liked the idea of a photo essay. She also loved soccer. She decided her photo essay would be about a soccer game. Talia asked her dad if she could use his phone to take pictures.

The next day, Talia went to a soccer game some of her friends were playing in. Talia took pictures of her friends warming up. She got a nice shot of Franny and Jasmine running. She got another shot of Maria scoring a goal.

Capturing photos of moving objects or people can be trickier than taking photos of things that are still.

Talia also took pictures of a dandelion growing on the field. She zoomed in to show the details of the grass and dandelion.

When Talia got home, her dad helped her upload the pictures to his computer. Then she printed them. She put her pictures in a book so she could share them with her teacher.

What Is Photography?

Photography is a visual art form. It involves capturing light to create still images called photographs, or photos. A person who takes photos is known as a photographer.

Some people take photos to capture important moments in time. Others use photography to express creativity. Photographers use a variety of styles and

Why Is It Called Photography?

The word *photography* comes from two Greek words. One is *phōtós*. The other is *graphein*. Together, they translate to mean "drawing with light." The first time the word *photography* was used was in the 1830s.

People can take photographs anywhere, including underwater.

techniques to take photos. People around the world take photos every day. Photography is an art form with many possibilities.

Explore Online

Visit the website below. Does it give any new information about taking photos that wasn't in Chapter One?

Photography

abdocorelibrary.com/art-of-photography

Camera lenses come in different sizes. Short lenses are good for wide-angle shots. Long lenses are better for close-up shots.

CHAPTER 2

Taking Photographs

Photos are taken by pointing a camera at a subject. The camera's lens focuses on the subject. A lens is made of glass plates inside a casing. It captures light. That light is then directed toward a single point and becomes a photo.

Photographs can be captured on **film** or digitally. Photographers use a variety of tools to create unique images. Devices called filters can change the color of a photograph. Different-sized lenses allow people to zoom in on or out from a subject. Tripods are stands that help keep cameras still.

Types of Cameras

Some cameras use film to capture photographs. One side of the film is covered in light-sensitive material. When people take a picture, they press a button that exposes the film to light. This creates a reversed version of the image on the film. That reversed image is known as a negative.

Polaroid cameras are a popular type of camera. They are known as instant cameras, meaning the photo develops right after it is taken.

Once a roll of film is used, it cannot be used to take more photographs. Photographers must then **develop** the photos. This is done in a darkroom. A darkroom is a room that uses a special red light. This prevents the light-sensitive film from being destroyed. Photographers use a chemical process to turn a negative into a finished photo. They do not know what the image looks like until it is developed.

Parts of a DSLR Camera

All DSLR cameras have the same basic parts. But some DSLRs have more settings than others.

Digital cameras also capture light. But they do not use film. Instead, they use a light-sensitive **sensor**. A computer inside the camera turns information from the sensor into an image. A popular type of digital camera is called a digital single lens reflex (DSLR).

Digital cameras create a finished photo right away. Most digital cameras have a viewing screen. Photographers can look at their image right after it is taken. Digital cameras also electronically store images on a memory card. Memory cards can hold thousands of images at once.

Camera Obscura

The camera obscura was an early device that was used to capture images. It showed an image on one side of a dark space. This was done by using a tiny opening where light could come through. In 1802, inventor Thomas Wedgwood shone an image onto a piece of paper **treated** with chemicals. The chemicals prevented Wedgwood's picture from fading.

Many professional photographers use a bag to carry their equipment to prevent damaging it.

Some people use **software** such as Photoshop to **edit** digital images. This allows people to create images that are not possible to take naturally. Photographers may make a photo lighter or darker. Or they may change the color of an object in the photo.

Photography Styles

There are many styles of photography. Landscape photographs are horizontal.

Food photographers aim to capture how good food looks and tastes through their cameras.

Portrait photos are vertical. Panoramic photos capture very wide-angle images.

Photographers may capture different kinds of images. These could be anything from sports events to weddings. Some people take photographs of nature or food. Or they might take fashion photographs.

Shooting in a studio allows photographers to control different elements of their photos, such as the lighting and backdrop.

Photos can be taken in black and white or in color. Some people may edit their photos to be in both color and black and white. In a studio, photographers shine lights on their subjects to achieve different effects. Photographers working with natural sunlight may take photos at certain times of day. They can also shoot the same subject from different angles.

Further Evidence

Look at the website below. Does it give any new evidence to support Chapter Two?

How Does a Camera Work?

abdocorelibrary.com/art-of-photography

The daguerreotype was one of the earliest forms of photography. It was invented in 1839 by Louis Daguerre.

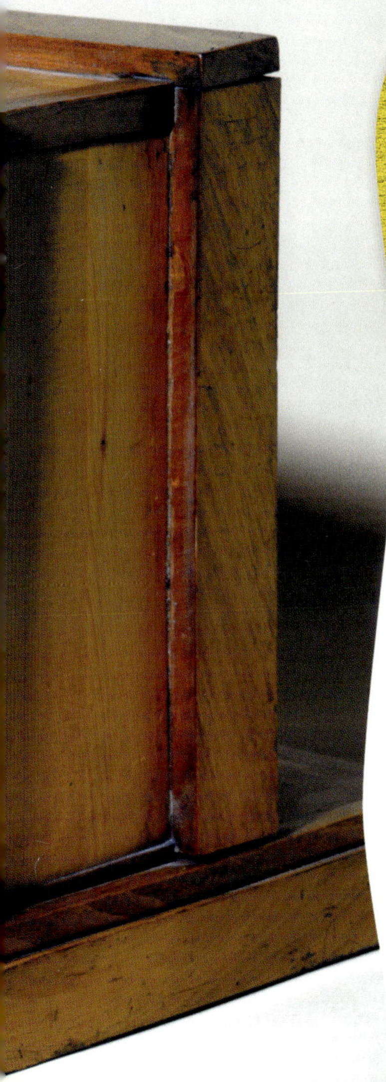

CHAPTER 3

The Influence of Photography

The oldest surviving photograph was taken in 1826. It was captured by a man named Nicéphore Niépce. The photo was of his garden taken from the window of his home. Niépce called the photo "View from a Window at Le Gras."

Subjects in early photographs had to be still. Because of this, early photographs did not include people. The first photo with people in it was taken in 1839 by Louis Daguerre. The first color photograph was taken in 1861 by Thomas Sutton. It was a picture of a ribbon. Color film was introduced in 1942 by the company Kodak.

Famous Photographers

Many people have used photography to create amazing art. Dorothea Lange was a documentary photographer. She took photographs of people during a period called the Great Depression (1929–1939). Lange's most famous photograph is of a mother and her three children. It is called "Migrant Mother."

Many photographs by Dorothea Lange, *pictured*, are featured in museums across the United States.

Ansel Adams was known for his landscape photography. Many of his photos were of US national parks. Adams used his photographs to promote environmental causes.

Annie Leibovitz is a portrait photographer. She is most known for taking photographs of celebrities. Leibovitz worked for the magazine *Rolling Stone* in the 1970s. Her creative pictures helped make the magazine famous.

Neil Leifer is considered one of the best sports photographers. He captures action shots of athletes. He also takes their portraits. One of Leifer's most famous photographs is of boxer Muhammad Ali, taken in 1964. It shows Ali standing over an opponent he had just knocked down.

Mathew Brady

Mathew Brady was one of the first famous US photographers. He took many well-known photographs of the American Civil War (1861–1865). In 1862, Brady displayed photographs he took of the Battle of Antietam. These photos allowed people to see for the first time how horrible wars could be.

Art museums often have exhibits that showcase different photographers' works or certain types of photos.

Museums and Festivals

There are hundreds of photography museums around the world. One famous museum is the International Center of Photography (ICP). It is located in New York City. The ICP has more than 200,000 photographs. It also hosts the Infinity Awards. This is an awards show that honors achievements in photography.

Today, many people share their photos on social media or on websites.

Some photographers show their work at photography festivals. Les Rencontres d'Arles in France features works by new and famous photographers. The Fix Photo Festival takes place in London, England. It features a photo contest that anyone can join.

Great photographs can be captured in many ways. They are also enjoyed by people around the world. People of all ages and skill levels can take photographs.

Primary Source

Henri Cartier-Bresson was a famous French photographer during the 1900s. He is best known for capturing photos of everyday life in a style called street photography. Cartier-Bresson said:

> It is an **illusion** that photos are made with the camera . . . they are made with the eye, heart, and head.

Source: Terrill Bodner. "Using the Eye, Heart and Head in Photography." *Medium*, 20 Oct. 2023, medium.com. Accessed 18 Apr. 2024.

What's the Big Idea?

What is this quote's main idea? Explain how the main idea is supported by details.

Art Supplies

Camera

Tripod

Film roll

Photo editing software

Memory card

Glossary

develop
to turn a negative into a finished photograph

edit
to change or correct something

film
a thin strip of plastic that captures images

illusion
a false idea or belief

sensor
a device that measures and records something

software
programs that are used on a computer

treated
coated with material meant to protect or preserve

Online Resources

To learn more about photography, visit our free resource websites below.

Core Library CONNECTION
FREE! COMMON CORE MULTIMEDIA RESOURCES

Visit **abdocorelibrary.com** or scan this QR code for free Common Core resources for teachers and students, including vetted activities, multimedia, and booklinks, for deeper subject comprehension.

Booklinks NONFICTION NETWORK
FREE! ONLINE NONFICTION RESOURCES

Visit **abdobooklinks.com** or scan this QR code for free additional online weblinks for further learning. These links are routinely monitored and updated to provide the most current information available.

Learn More

Murray, Julie. *Camera*. Abdo, 2023.

Reed, Darcy. *Extraordinary Women with Cameras*. Rocky Nook, 2022.

Shaw, Mary. *The Art of Film*. Abdo, 2025.

Index

About the Author

David J. Clarke is a freelance writer. Originally from Helena, Montana, he now lives in Savannah, Georgia.